Contents

Self-Management ✓

This is me …

Words to describe me …

What are five things you'd like to share about yourself?

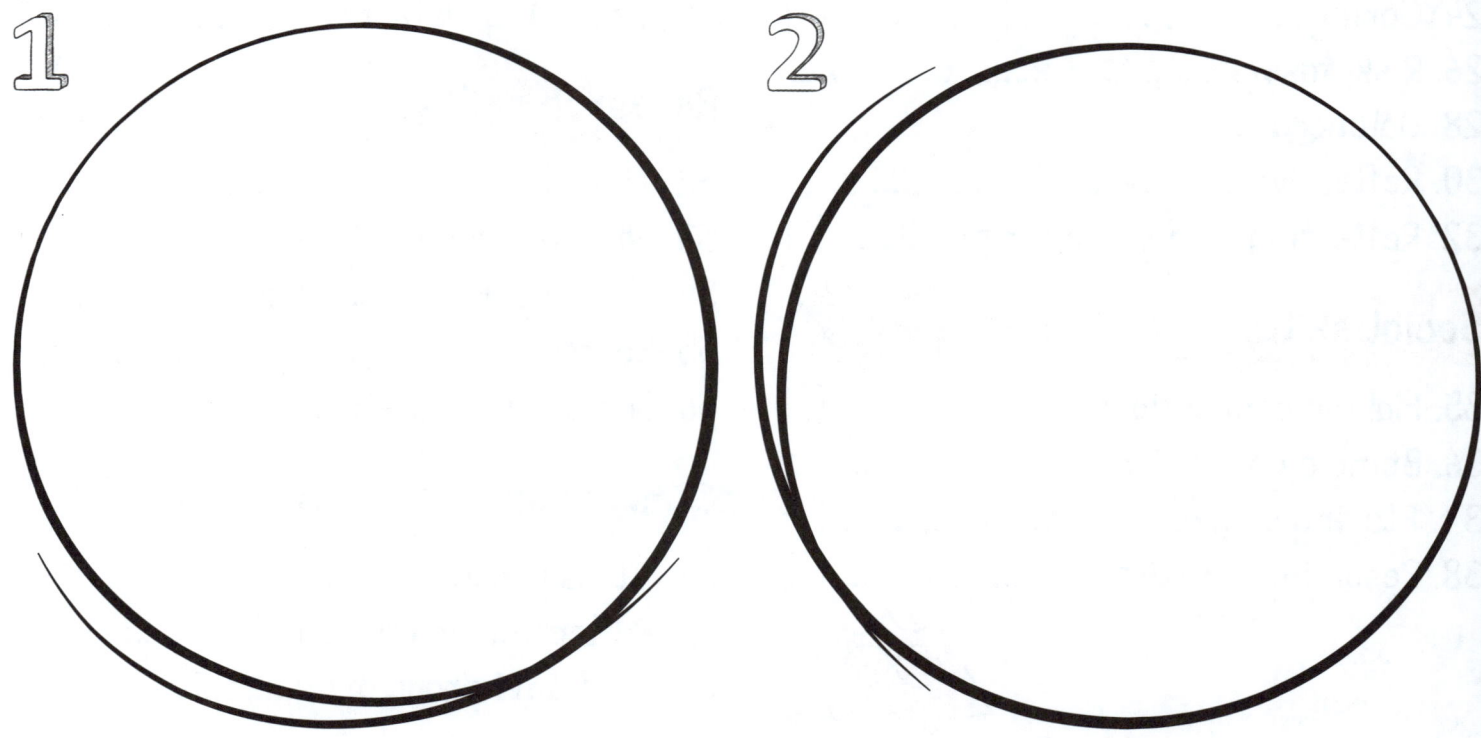

1

2

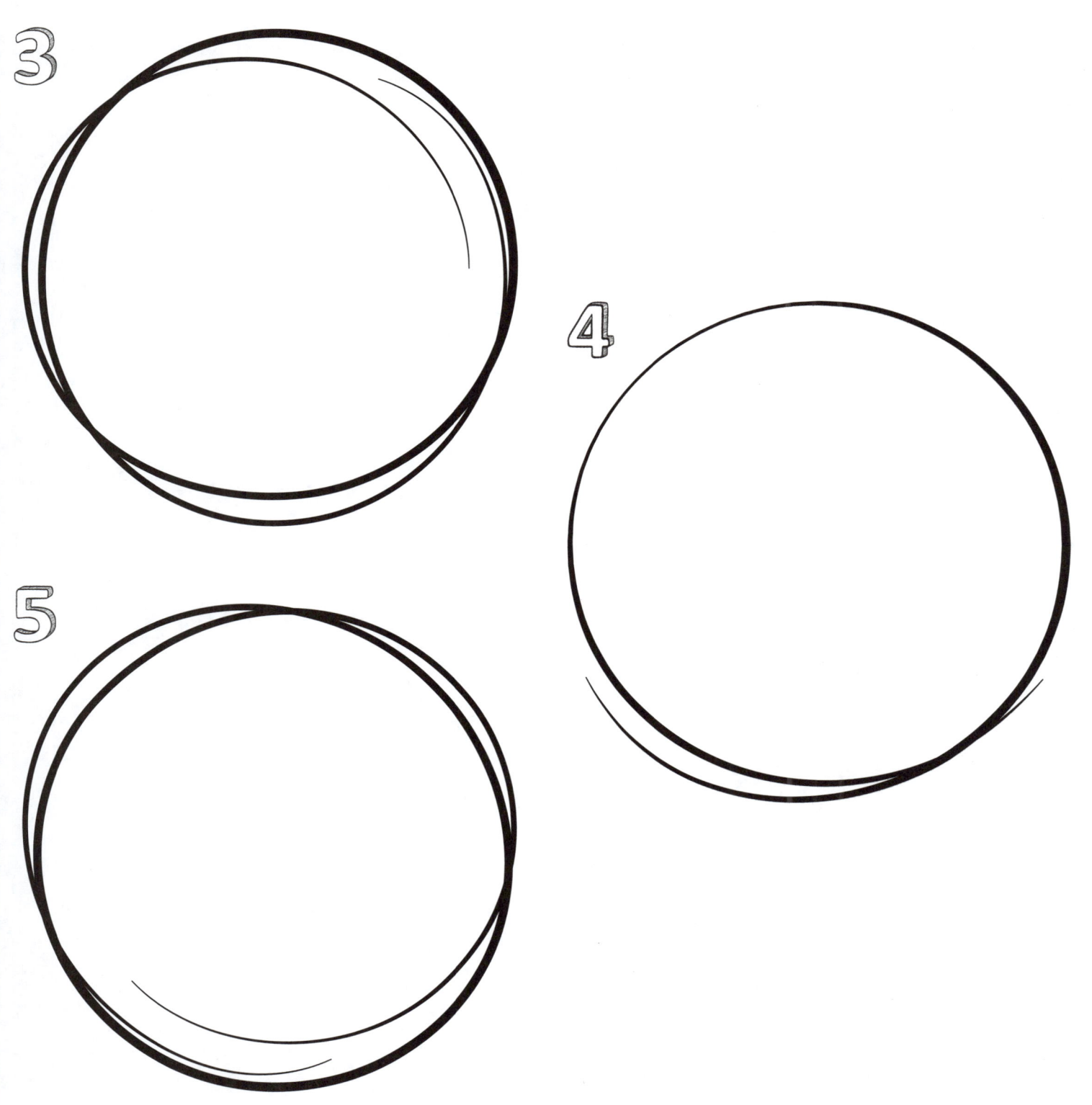

💬 Share with a partner.

What do you notice? What makes you special?

My strengths

I'm good at …

I'm getting better at …

 How are we different to others? How are we the same?

Which animal best describes you as a learner?

I like to take my time.

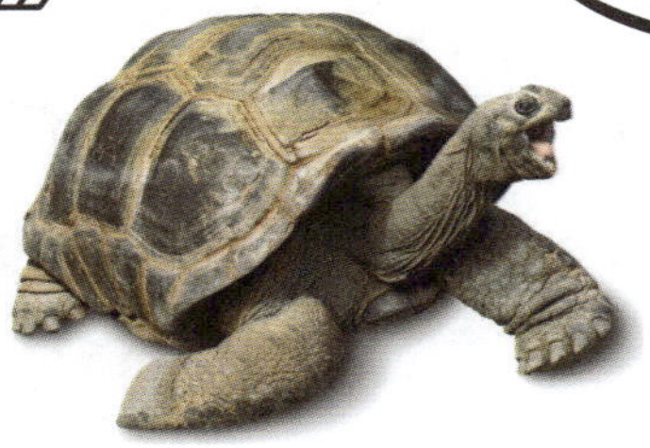

I have lots of energy.

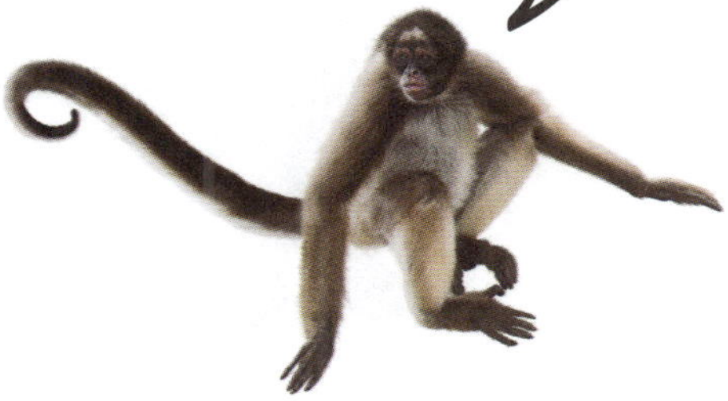

I know a lot of facts.

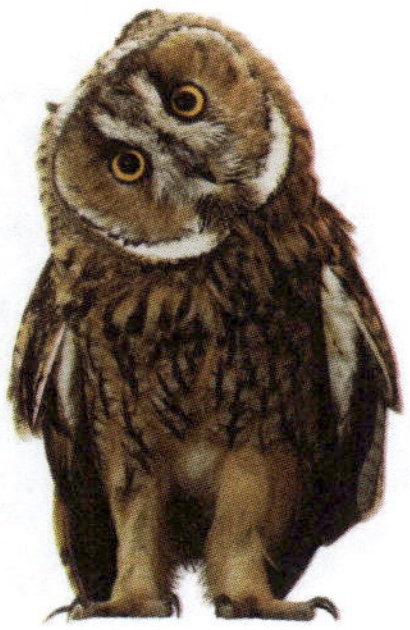

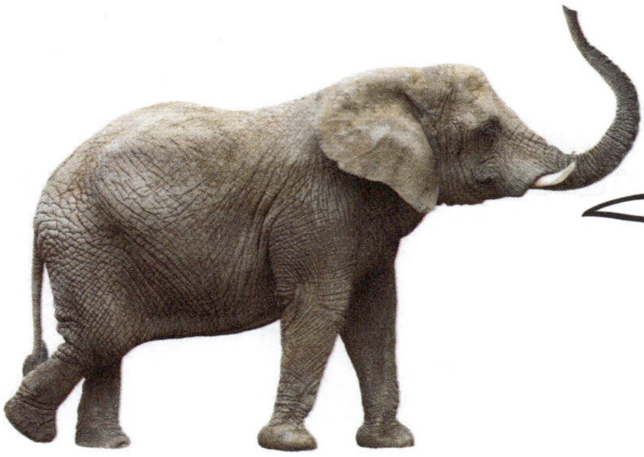

I sort out problems.

What other animal are you like? Draw it here.

I chose the ....

because ....

....

Discuss your ideas with a partner.

Growth mindset

How can having a growth mindset help you as a learner?

....

....

....

....

What have you recently learned to do?

....

....

....

....

My goals

Choose one goal you would like to reach this year.
Draw it on the label.

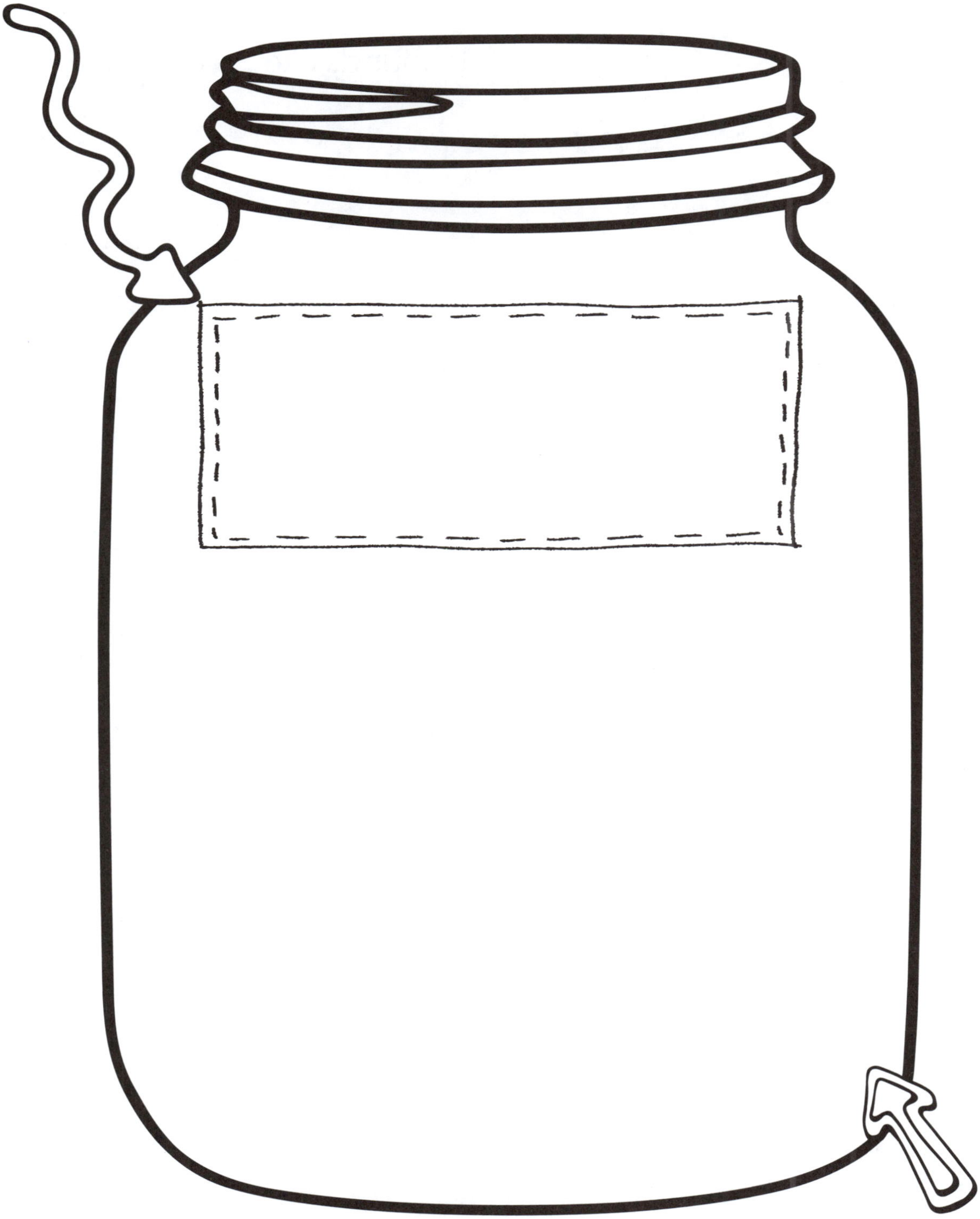

Draw or write ways you can
reach your goal inside the jar.

7

Use your senses to describe your classroom.
What can you see, hear and feel?

It looks like …	It sounds like …

It feels like …

 What would you like to add or take away from your classroom?

Think about your classroom. What helps you to be a good learner?
Add your ideas.

What makes me feel safe and supported at school?

How can we make sure everyone feels respected?

How can we create a positive feeling in the classroom?

Our Essential Agreements

Essential agreements help to keep the class safe and happy.
They show how **caring** we can be.

What essential agreements are important to you?

 Where are the essential agreements in your classroom?

Think about the essential agreements. Decide which will be easy for you to follow, and which you might need reminding about.

Agreements I will find easy to follow ...

Agreements I might need reminding about ...

How can you help your classmates follow the agreements?

Inquirer

What does an **inquirer** do? Add your ideas.

I ask questions.

Read about being an **inquirer** …

Snail finds out that someone has eaten all the bugs! He decides to find out who did it.

Snail explores his whole world, looking for answers …

Be an **inquirer**.

Stick a picture connected to your unit of inquiry here.

What do you see, think and wonder?

I see …

I think …

I wonder …

Knowledgeable

How can you be **knowledgeable**? Add your ideas.

> I know a lot.

Read about being **knowledgeable** …

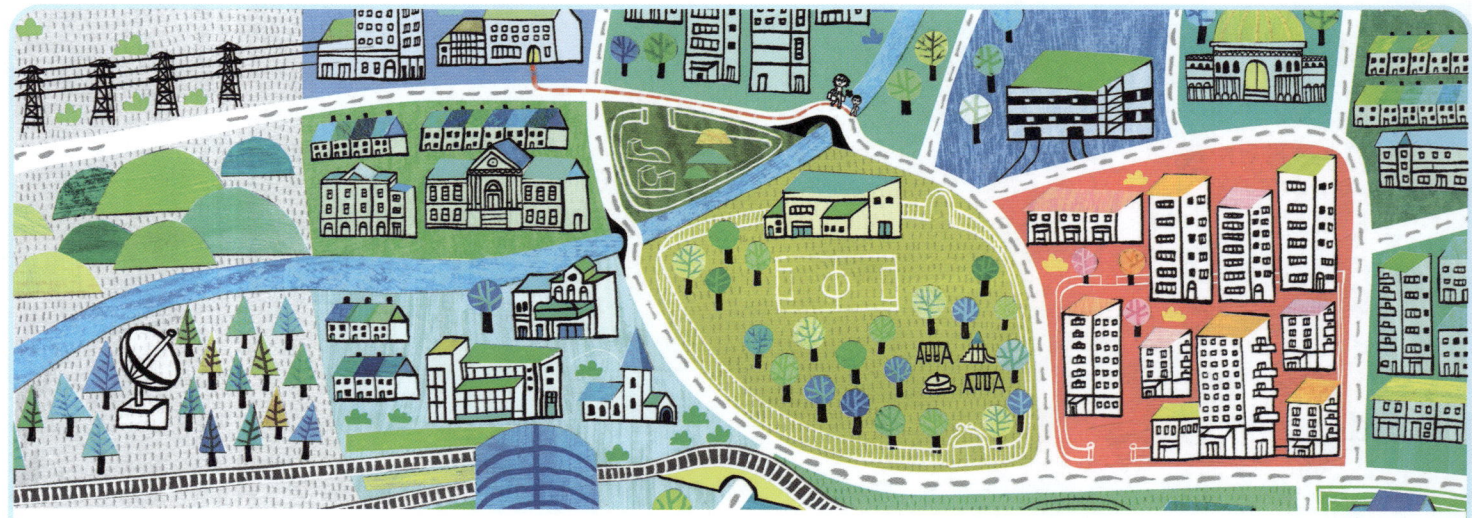

Martha loves to learn things.

She also loves to make maps like this one to share her knowledge.

Be **knowledgeable**.

What do you know lots about?

 Numbers? Words? Facts?

Draw and write some fun facts that you can share with a partner.

> Did you know ...

 How can we share our knowledge with others?

Thinker

What does a **thinker** do? Add your ideas.

I use my head.

Read about being a **thinker** …

Circle wants to build a tower, but none of her ideas work.

Luckily, Circle is a good thinker and has one more idea …

Be a **thinker**. Pick an activity below.

Look at the counters.

How many different ways can you add them together to make the sum 12?

For example: 3 + 4 + 5 = 12

2   3   4

5   6   7

8

Write your ideas here:

Look at Teddy's clothes.

How many different outfits can Teddy wear with these clothes?

Write or draw your ideas here:

What steps did you follow? Did your partner follow the same steps?

Communicator

What does a **communicator** do? Add your ideas.

> I share my ideas.

Read about being a **communicator** …

The otters and badgers were **not** friends. They lived on different sides of a river and never met.

> Why can't we just share it all?

Francie the otter used her skills as a communicator. She brought the otters and badgers together and they all shared cakes.

Be a **communicator**.

Ask your classmates if they know how to say 'hello' in another language.

Do you know how to say 'hello' in another way?

 How can we say 'hello' without using words?

Principled

How can you be **principled**? Add your ideas.

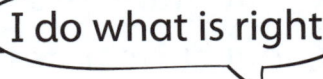
I do what is right.

Read about being **principled** …

Stella is worried when her friend, the seagull, keeps bringing her bits of plastic.

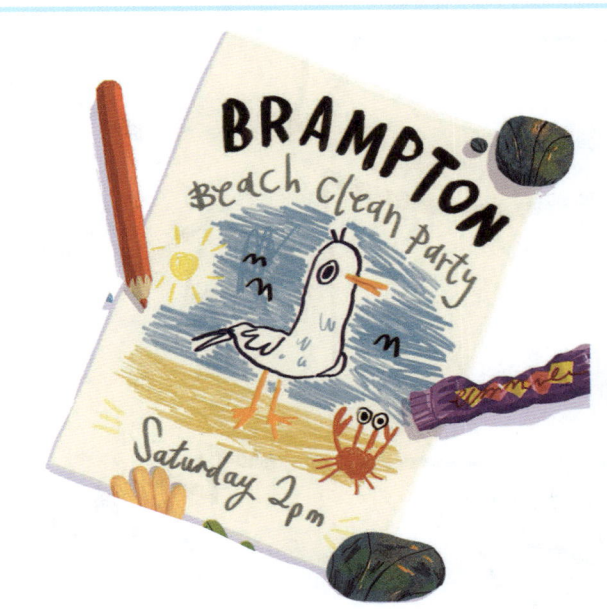

Stella organizes a beach clean to help her friend.

Be **principled**.

Playing games fairly teaches us to treat others with respect.

Play a game with some classmates.

Be a **communicator** and explain the rules of the game carefully.

I showed respect by …

Why is it important to be **principled**?

Did you follow the rules of the game?

Yes! ☐   Sort of ☐   No  ☐

 Open-minded

Open-minded

How can you be **open-minded**? Add your ideas.

I listen to others' ideas.

Read about being **open-minded** …

The fruits and vegetables were always fighting.

We're open-minded – we're friends!

Let's give peace a chance.

We will if you will.

When everyone saw Grape and Mushroom being friends, the fighting stopped.

Be **open-minded**.

Bring something that shows your culture to share with your class.

Draw it here …

How do objects like this help us learn about others?

What did I learn about my classmates?

Caring

How can you be **caring**? Add your ideas.

I am kind.

Read about being **caring** ...

There are lots of ways to be caring. You can smile, say hello and share with others.

You can be caring to nature and animals. You can be caring to yourself, too!

What are some ways you can be **caring** at school?

 How can we be **caring** in our local community?

Risk-taker

How can you be a **risk-taker**? Add your ideas.

I try new things.

Read about being a **risk-taker** ...

Hop can't ride a bike. He keeps falling off.

Hop is a risk-taker. He gets back on his bike and keeps trying until he can ride!

When I was younger, I was scared to …

Now I am older, I can …

Here I am, being a risk-taker …

Being a risk-taker makes me feel

 How can you help others when they feel scared?

Balanced

How can you be **balanced**? Add your ideas.

I take care of myself.

Read about being **balanced** …

'Hurry up,' shouted the bus driver. 'I'm running late.'

Everyone tells Tisha to hurry up, but she just wants to slow down!

Slowing down helps Tisha to be balanced. She can enjoy time with her family and notice everything around her.

Draw things that you enjoy at school.

Inside …

Outside …

With friends …

By myself …

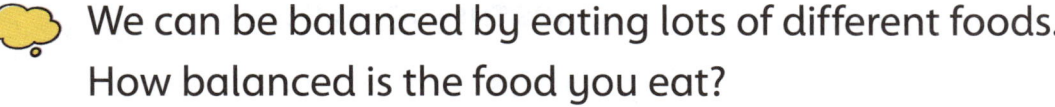 We can be balanced by eating lots of different foods.
How balanced is the food you eat?

Reflective

How can you be **reflective**? Add your ideas.

I think of how to be better.

Read about being **reflective** ...

Sunny and his dad have moved to a new place. They reflect on how they miss their old home.

They spend time looking at birds that remind them of home. This makes them feel better.

Think of a time when there has been an argument at school.

 With a partner, act out the argument.

How could it have been sorted out?

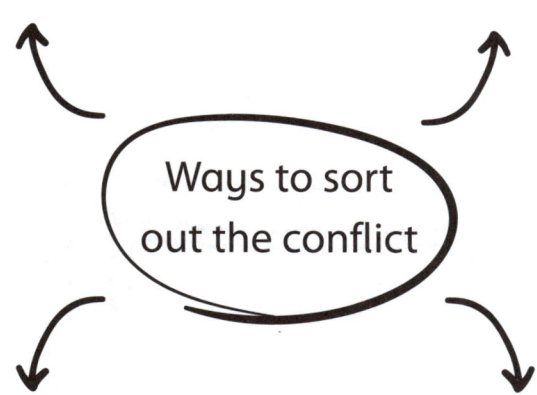

Ways to sort
out the conflict

Reflecting on my learner profile

Draw pictures of yourself showing each learner profile attribute.

Inquirer
I ask questions.

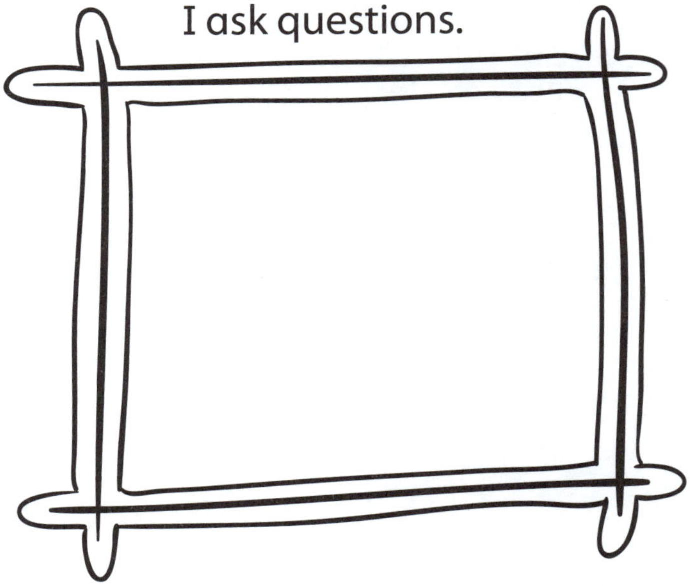

Knowledgeable
I know a lot.

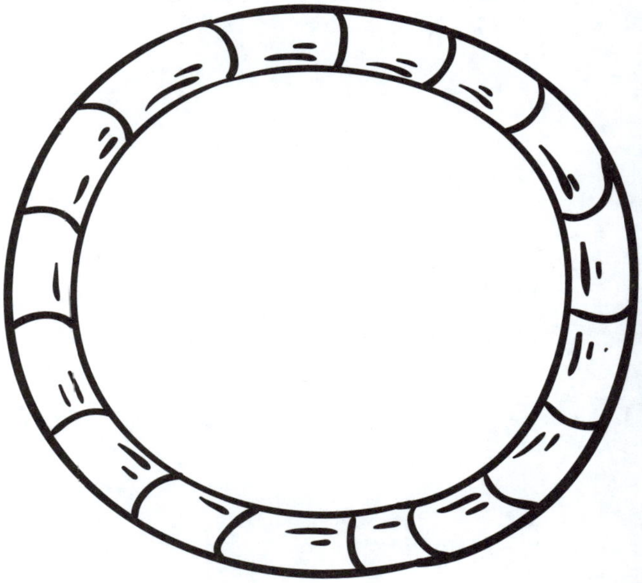

Thinker
I think deeply.

Principled
I do what is right.

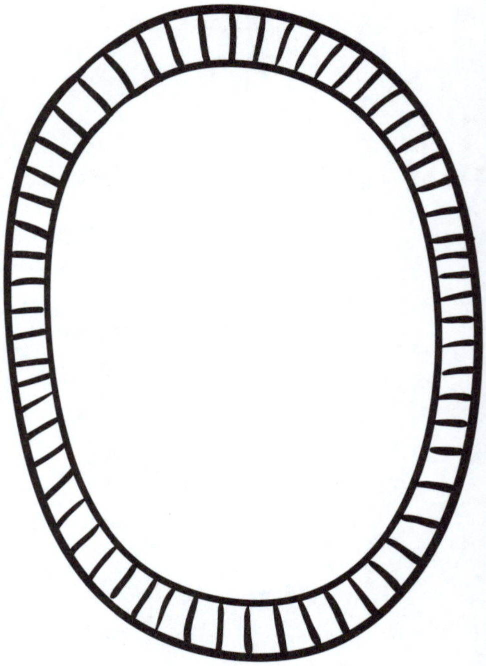

Communicator
I share my ideas.

Open-minded
I listen to others' ideas.

Caring
I am kind.

Risk-taker
I try new things.

Balanced
I take care of myself.

Reflective
I think of how to be better.

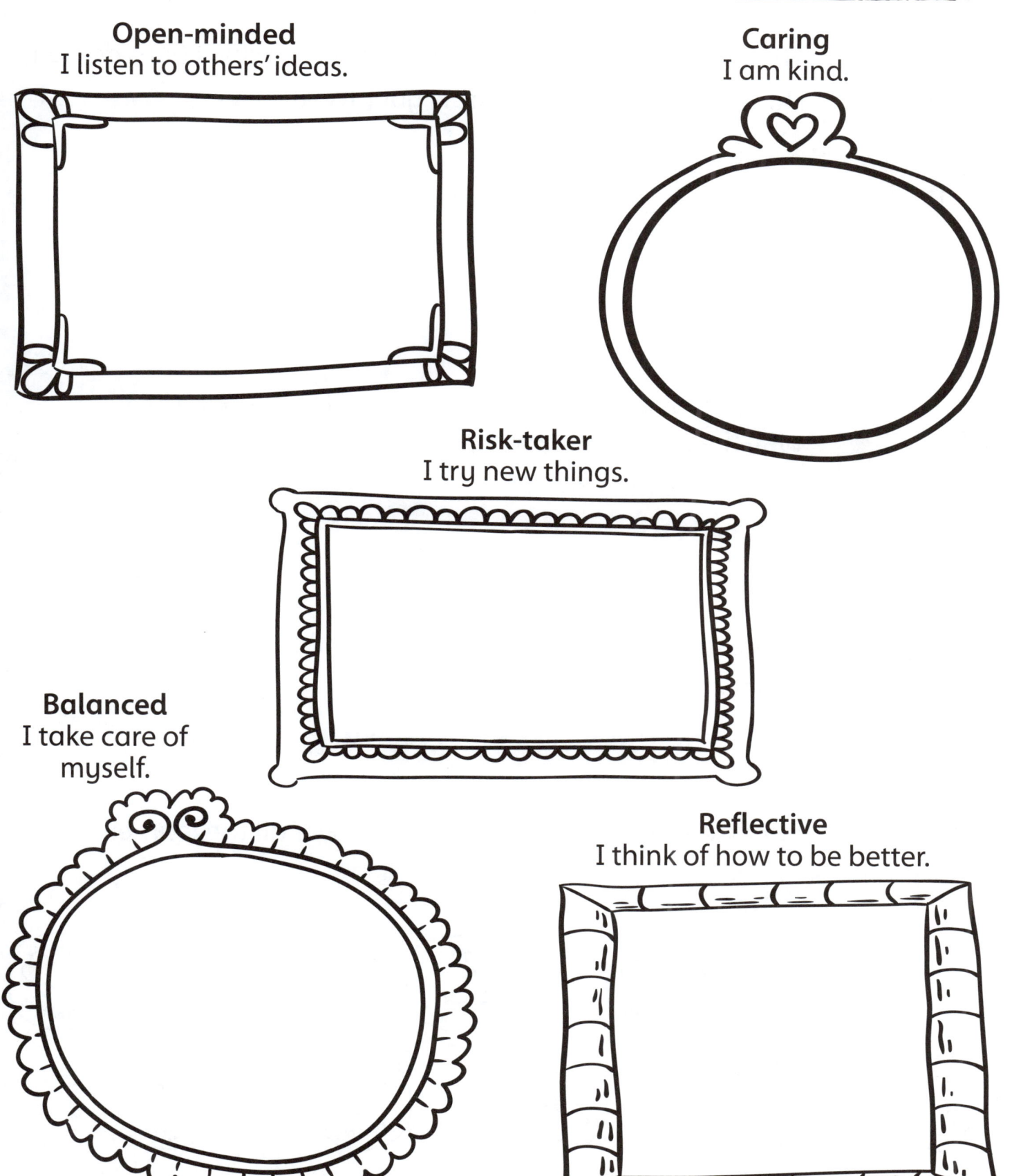

Reflecting on my learner profile

Think

Think about the learner profile attributes. Which ones do you show the most? Write or draw your top 3.

Pair

Talk to a partner. Compare your top 3 with their top 3. Which are the same? Which are different? Why might this be?

Share

Share your ideas with the rest of the class. Can you find any connections?

 Look at your essential agreements. Do they cover all the learner profile attributes?

Sit with a partner. Talk about your interests, hobbies, likes and dislikes.

Listen carefully and ask questions.

Use the circles below to write what you found out.

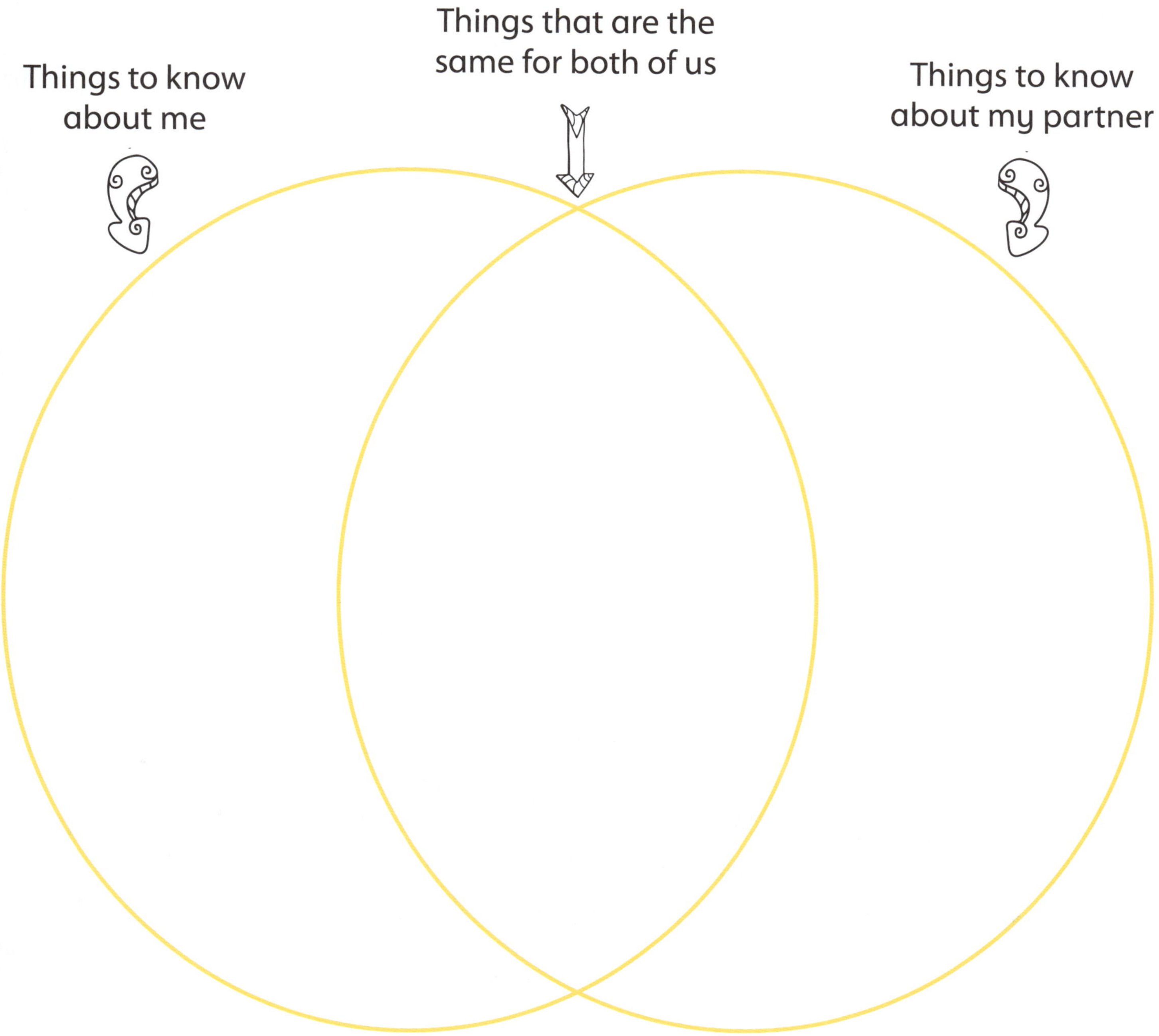

Things that are the
same for both of us

Things to know
about me

Things to know
about my partner

 How can we use this information to be more **caring** and build
stronger relationships?

Being a good friend

What makes a good friend? Write your ideas.

Think about these questions.

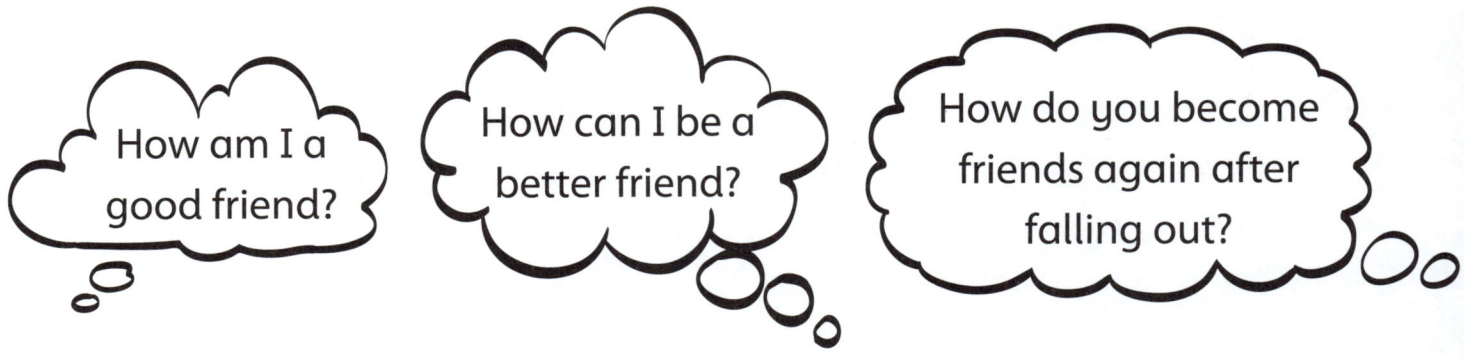

How am I a good friend?

How can I be a better friend?

How do you become friends again after falling out?

 What could you do to make a friend feel cared for?

Playing games

Playing games can be a lot of fun. You can learn many things when you play with others.

What are your favourite games to play with others?

My favourite game is

I also like to play …

 Share with a partner. See what games you both like to play.

Resolving conflict

Disagreeing with others can be upsetting.
Draw how conflict makes you feel.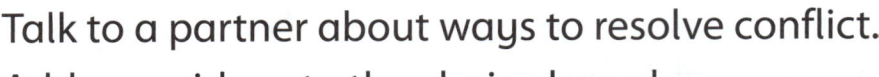

Talk to a partner about ways to resolve conflict.
Add more ideas to the choice board.

How can I resolve conflict? My choice board

Apologize

Share

 Which ideas would you find easy?
Which ideas would you find harder?
How could choice boards be used in your classroom?

Making choices

Do you know what you need help with and what you *don't* need help with? Knowing this helps you to become a more **reflective** learner.

I don't need help when I …

This makes me feel …

I need help when I …

This makes me feel …

 Talk to a partner about why you think this.

 How can you help others with activities they find hard?

What makes you happy? What makes you sad?

Write or draw what makes you feel each emotion.

☺ Happy

☹ Sad

😮 Excited

☺ Calm

😣 Angry

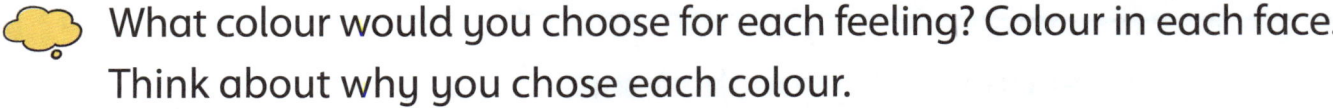 What colour would you choose for each feeling? Colour in each face.

Think about why you chose each colour.

Compare your answers with a partner.

My happy place

Close your eyes. Think of the place where you feel most happy and safe.
What does it look like? What does it feel like? What does it smell like?
Draw and write about your happy place.

 Talk to a partner and explain why this is your happy place.

What is well-being?

How do these pictures show well-being?

 How do you look after yourself? Discuss with a partner.

Well-being checklist

Today, I feel …

☺ ☐   😌 ☐   😐 ☐   ☹ ☐   😣 ☐

I drank enough water today …

I ate breakfast today …

I moved my body today …

Yes ☐
No ☐

Yes ☐
No ☐

Yes ☐
No ☐

Today, I will do this to help my well-being …

Some signs have pictures. The pictures give us information. We can understand them without needing words.

What might these signs mean?

Draw some signs that you have seen.

 Share with a partner. Do you have any that are the same?

Explain what each sign means.

Discuss as a class. Could signs be used in your classroom?

Understanding body language

We can use our bodies to communicate non-verbally (without using words).

Write or draw some action words in the boxes (run, laugh …).

Use your action words to play charades. Act out each action to a partner.
Can they guess what the action is?

Were you a good **communicator** during this game?

Yes ☐ No ☐ Why? ....

What did you find easy? What was hard?

Being a good listener and speaker

To be a good **communicator**, you need to be good at listening and speaking. This can take practice.

1 Let's play the GUESS WHAT game!
Draw pictures of simple things here (animals, objects, food …).

2 Take it in turns to describe something you have drawn to a partner.
You can talk about what colour it is, how big it is, if it is alive or not …
Can your partner guess what it is?

Was this game easy or hard? Why?
Are you a better listener or speaker?

As a class, create some essential agreements for group work.

1 Use this mind map to think of ideas.

2 Think about all types of communication skills: speaking, listening, reading and writing.

Our essential agreements for group work

3 Share your ideas.

4 Decide on the essential agreements for group work.

Wondering

Being a critical thinker means being an **inquirer** and asking good questions. This helps you make better decisions.

Look at this house.

Think of some questions using these sentence starters …

Why …

What if …

How …

 Share your questions with a partner.
How could you find the answers?

The yes or no game

1 Read these questions.

2 Draw arrows from the questions to the Yes – No line.

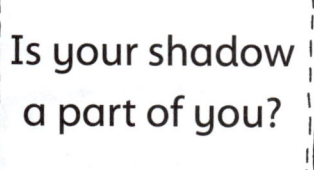
Is your shadow a part of you?

Will this plant live?
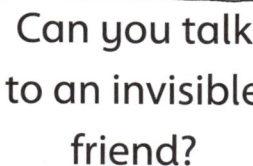

Can you talk to an invisible friend?

Yes ⬅——————————————➡ No

Maybe

Write some of your own yes or no questions.

....

....

....

....

....

....

....

 Ask a partner your questions. Do you agree with their answers?

This is an ordinary stick … or is it?
Use your imagination to think of
another use for it! Could it be a
walking stick? Or a climbing frame for ants?
Draw your ideas below.

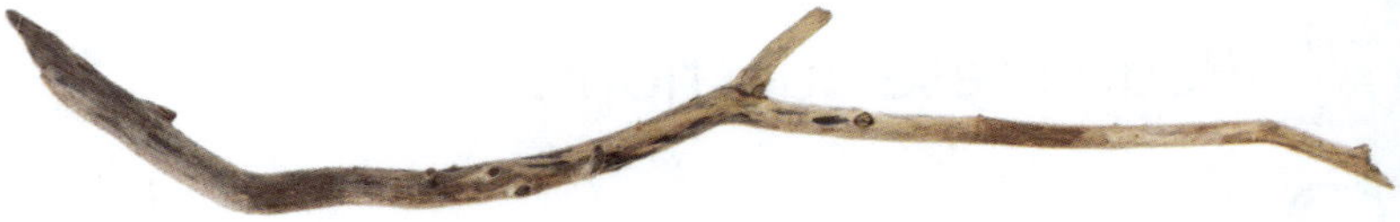

 Share your ideas with a partner. What is similar or different?

Reflecting on your week will help you find out what you are good at and what you might need to work on.

This week, I mostly felt …

☺ ☐   😌 ☐   😐 ☐   ☹ ☐   😣 ☐

My favourite activity was …

I am most proud of …

This week, I learned …

Next week, I will …

Choose an additional concept from your inquiry and write it here.

Use the boxes below to think about the concept.

See it! Draw some pictures to show what you think about it.

Feel it! How does it make you feel?

Ask it! What questions do you want to ask about it?

Show it! Choose a picture or word that explains the main idea.

What is the most important?

Sorting and ordering helps you to think about what is important and what is not as important. We practise these skills to become better **thinkers**.

What is the most important thing for your well-being?

- healthy food
- family
- friends
- sleep
- water
- exercise

Put these things in order from most to least important.

most ➡
important

least
important
⬇

 Share and compare your answers with a partner.

Thinking about questions

We can ask questions using different question words.
These help us to find out different types of information.

Find a picture of something that interests you.
Think of some questions about the picture.

Who? What? When? Where? How? Why?

Where could you find the answers to your questions?

- ▢ books
- ▢ online
- ▢ my teacher
- ▢ other

Sources of information

Finding information from lots of places helps to make your research **balanced**.

Below are some sources where you can get information.

Circle a number from 1 to 10 to show how confident you are with the source.

Not confident   Confident

Talking to others

1   2   3   4   5   6   7   8   9   10

Reading books

1   2   3   4   5   6   7   8   9   10

Searching the internet

1   2   3   4   5   6   7   8   9   10

Watching videos

1   2   3   4   5   6   7   8   9   10

Share your thoughts with a partner.

Can you trust all information that you find? How do you know?

Sustainable Development Goals

People all around the world have made a list of 17 goals. They are to help our planet and its people.

Here are the first two goals:

We should all have money for basic needs, like food, water and a place to live.

We should all have enough food.

Why are these goals important?

What do you wonder?

 Discuss your thoughts with a partner.

Class project: Making a calm space

School is a busy place. Sometimes we need a space to relax, calm down or spend time together.

Your challenge: Design and create a calm space that brings people together. Use the PLAN action steps to organize your ideas.

P What is the problem?
Why do you need this space?

Where can we make our calm space?

Look around your classroom and think about places that could be a calm space. Draw them below.

List your ideas.

 # Coming up with ideas

Problem-solvers manage their emotions and think creatively.
They keep going until they find an answer. They love challenges!

Write a list of things you would like to have in the class calm space.
Things to think about …

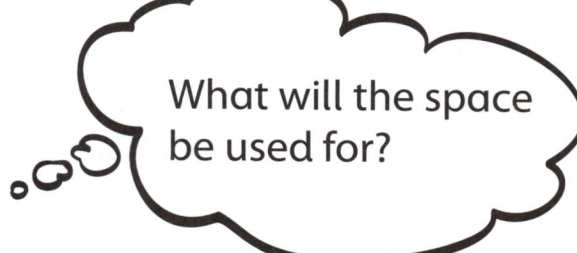

What will the space be used for?

Will essential agreements be created for the space?

....

....

....

....

....

....

....

....

 Share your ideas with a partner. Are any of your ideas the same?

 **Taking action**

The best ideas come when we work together, ask questions and find solutions.

 **Action steps**

Write what your job will be.

....

....

....

Write your action steps.

I need to ...

I can do this by ...

I need to ...

I can do this by ...

 As a class, share ideas and make an action plan.

Taking time to reflect

N Notice your success! | Score how successful you were from 1 to 5 (1 = not very successful, 5 = very successful).

The tricky part was …

I learned how to …

This helped me understand …

I still need to work on …

Where else might you need a calm space? Draw it here.

Reflecting on my year

Something I learned …

Something I am proud of …

The learner profile attribute
that I used the most was …

The book I loved
the most …

A memory I'll keep …

Next year, I hope to …

How have you changed this year?

I used to …

Now I can …

 How do you feel when you reflect on your year?

63

What am I proud of?

Write a letter to yourself to explain everything you are proud of.